What others are saying about this book:

"...an immensely valuable book that provides a 'natural' way of bringing up and discussing the many difficult issues concerning divorce... it helped the conversation focus on my child's concerns and feelings. A tremendous source of information and comfort during a rather difficult time." — **Faith Roberts, divorced parent, communications specialist, Denver, Colorado.**

"...this book certainly accomplishes the author's purpose: to cushion youngsters' hearts and lives as they move through the painful experience of adjusting to their parents' divorce...parents, teachers and counselors will welcome this book." — **Sister Regina Alfonso, SND, Ed.M., Assistant Professor of Education, Notre Dame College of Ohio.**

"...it hits the heart of the matter and offers excellent explanations and support for adults as well as children...attorneys should give this book to the parents at the time the divorce is filed." — **Marilyn Golub Weisenborn, divorced parent, educational secretary, Houston, Texas.**

"This book is just what children of divorced families need...it is a magnificent book which will bring the reader much help and assurance." — **Br. James King, TOR, Boston. Mass.**

"...Prokop has concisely defined the most common worries children experience during divorce. In simple language he has been able to state their fears and explain why they are just that, fears...a great comfort to children while they learn to cope with and adjust to their new family life." — **Carolyn Chapman, M.S., divorced parent, teacher, San Diego City Schools, San Diego, California.**

"...insightful, grasps the concerns and confusions of 'divorced' children, provides warm support, understanding and reassurance..." — **Edward Amicucci, Ph.D., counseling psychologist, Associated Psychiatrists, Youngstown, Ohio**

This book belongs to

_____,

a nice kid.

DIVORCE HAPPENS TO THE NICEST KIDS

A Self Help Book for Kids (3-15) and Adults

Michael S. Prokop, M.Ed., School Psychologist

Illustrated by Dennis J. McCullough

Kaya Books ©

Alegra House Publishers, Warren, Ohio

DIVORCE HAPPENS TO THE NICEST KIDS

A Self Help Book for Kids (3-15) and Adults

Michael S. Prokop, M.Ed.
Illustrated by Dennis J. McCullough

Published by:

Alegra House Publishers
Post Office Box 1443
Warren, Ohio 44482 U.S.A.

Kaya Books ©

Copyright ©1986 by Michael S. Prokop

Library of Congress Cataloging-in-Publication Data.

Prokop, Michael S.,
   Divorce Happens to the Nicest Kids

   "Kaya Books."
   Summary: Discussion questions and a brief story examine many of the common concerns and feelings that frequently accompany divorce.

   1. Children of divorced parents — Juvenile literature.

2. Divorce — Juvenile literature. (Psychology) — Juvenile literature. I. McCullough, Dennis J., HQ777.5.P76   1986   646.7'8 ISBN 0-933879-25-3 ISBN 0-933879-26-1 (pbk.)

3. Separation (1. Divorce) ill. II. Title. 85-72180

...About the author

Michael S. Prokop is currently a school psychologist with the Warren City Schools and Developmental Clinic of Warren, Ohio. He graduated with honors from Kent State University with a Bachelor's degree in Psychology and earned a Master's degree in School Psychology from Bowling Green State University. For the past eight years he has been providing individual and group psychotherapy for children with divorced and separated parents. He frequently lectures and provides workshops concerning divorce, relaxation therapy, and positive mental health. He lives in Cortland, Ohio and enjoys basketball, skiing, mountain climbing, and sailing.

Acknowledgements

I wish to express my deep and lasting appreciation to my family and to my friends and assistants who helped in the preparation of this book. A special "thank you" to the parents and children of divorce who shared their deepest hopes, fears, and experiences.

Information and professional assistance were contributed to this book by Sr. Mary C. Blooming, H.M.; Kathi Ciminero, B.S.; Matthew Ciminero; Joseph D. Consolino, M.A.; Sandy Consolino, M.A.; Marianne Cote, M.Ed.; Michael E. Donley; Edward Fiscus, Ph.D.; Michelle Fogarty, Dorothy Fogel, M.Ed.; George Gessner, J.D.; Linda Gessner, B.A.; Rev. M. Gerald Gordon, TOR; Natalie Hayes; Elizabeth Hoobler, M.A.; Louise Jones, R.N.; Sister Mary Jean Korejwo, SND; Sr. Susan Kurth, SND; Rev. Nino La Stella, TOR; Linda Marado; Sr. Mary Helene Minut, SND; Robert Phillips; Rachel Pool; Dan Poynter; Robert P. Prokop, M.Ed.; Gloria J. Province; Andrew Sattler, M.A.; Jan Smith, M.A.; Kathy Sparks, M.A.; Sr. Mary Janett Stamper, SND; Sr. Maribeth Rome, SND; Antoinette Ryan, B.S.; Carol Somerfeldt, M.Ed.; Beatrice Tallarico; Lisa Vecchione; Jan C. Wellman, M.A.; Mary White; and Carol J. Wilterdink.

Special thanks to Parents Without Partners #746; Myrna Warren, M.A., Editor; and Dan Marmion, Bob Bell, and Debra Hunkus for help with the graphics.

Contents

A Note to the Reader...

This book is designed to provide information regarding children and divorce. It is sold with the understanding that the publisher and author are not engaged in rendering legal or professional services. If legal or professional services are required, a competent professional should be sought.

The purpose of this book is not to reprint all information that is otherwise available to the author and publisher but to supplement and complement other texts. For more information, refer to the bibliography.

INTRODUCTION FOR ADULTS

The changes that divorce brings often cause children to feel anxious, angry, nervous, confused, guilty, lonely, and depressed. These unhealthy feelings are often caused by false beliefs that children have about divorce and themselves. It is not uncommon for children to worry about these false beliefs for months and even years. This often results in the above mentioned feelings as well as low grades in school, poor concentration skills, feelings of inferiority and low self worth.

Through years of research and providing psychotherapy for children, it became evident to me that many children who experience a divorce falsely believe the following: their inappropriate thoughts or actions are the cause of the divorce; divorce only happens to a few bad children; their thoughts have power over life events; their parents will reunite and marry each other again; they cannot be happy living with one parent; they cannot do well in school; divorce ruins the family; no one will take care of them after the divorce; and their parents don't love them anymore.

Through pain comes growth. Although divorce is usually a rather emotionally painful time for children, the divorce experience can be a time for children (and parents) to learn appropriate ways to cope with life's problems. By taking a close look at a child's thoughts, an adult can usually determine if they are based on fact or false beliefs. By exploring and understanding the realities of divorce, children can more readily cope with the truth and make appropriate adjustments.

It is my belief that children are rather resilient human beings who can deal effectively with life changes, such as divorce, when presented with the truth, knowledge, and given support. When children learn and believe this "fact of resiliency," rather than the unhealthy false beliefs previously mentioned, the healing process begins, self-confidence is enhanced, and coping skills develop.

The purpose of this book is to explain divorce in a truthful, honest, and simple manner so children may better understand divorce and themselves. This book may be used by parents, teachers, counselors, the clergy, social workers, and psychologists to help children understand their false beliefs concerning divorce and themselves. This new understanding may help diminish many unhealthy feelings and provide a sense of self worth, hope, and confidence.

HOW TO USE THIS BOOK

Some of the most common false beliefs that children have about divorce and themselves are listed on the following pages along with a true statement. It is recommended that the adult reviewing the book with the child make a note and discuss each point as it arises in the book. Page numbers are listed after each true statement to assist in this process.

It may prove helpful to review the false beliefs, true statements, and entire book a few times before reviewing the book with the child. This will help one feel comfortable with the concepts and ideas of the book.

This book has not been designed to be read and discussed in one sitting. Numerous sittings are recommended so the child may thoroughly absorb and understand the material.

Now, simply relax and begin enjoying the book. Good Luck.

Michael S. Prokop, M.Ed.
School Psychologist

FALSE BELIEFS AND TRUE STATEMENTS

FALSE BELIEF #1

Kids are the cause of the divorce.

TRUE STATEMENT

Kids are **not the cause** of the divorce and it is **not** their fault. Parents get divorced because they cannot work out their problems, are unhappy with each other, and no longer wish to live together. It is not because their kids have been bad, done something wrong, or have had evil thoughts. (Pages 92-93, 146-155)

FALSE BELIEF #2

Parents who get a divorce don't love their kids.

TRUE STATEMENT

Love is sometimes **hard to measure,** but most parents who get a divorce do love their kids very much. It is sometimes difficult for parents to show love for their kids when they are nervous and upset about the divorce. However, most parents do love their kids before, during, and after the divorce. (Pages 92-93, 124-125)

FALSE BELIEF #3

Some kids believe they will be abandoned and no one will take care of them after the divorce.

TRUE STATEMENT

Kids **are** taken care of even though their parents are divorced. After a divorce, most kids live with their mothers, but some kids live with their fathers. Also, just because one parent had to leave the home **doesn't** mean the remaining parent is going to leave or abandon the kids. (Pages 100-101, 126-127)

FALSE BELIEF #4

Some kids think that divorce ruins or destroys the family.

TRUE STATEMENT

Divorce **doesn't** ruin or destroy the family, it **changes** the family. Many things change the family such as illness, death, the birth of a child, and older children moving away to college or a job. Kids who have divorced parents still have two parents, one father and one mother, even though the parents no longer live together.

Specific changes families and kids may face after a divorce include living on less money, moving to a new neighborhood, changing schools and making new friends. (Pages 128-135)

FALSE BELIEF #5

Kids cannot be happy living with one parent.

TRUE STATEMENT

Kids **learn to adjust** to the changes in their families, which include divorce and living with one parent. They usually are happier a few months after the divorce because there is less fighting, angry words, confusion, and disorder in the home. (Pages 102-109, 130-135, 204-207)

FALSE BELIEF #6

Divorce only happens to a few bad kids.

TRUE STATEMENT

Just because a kid has divorced parents **doesn't** mean he or she is a bad person. It is unfortunate that parents get divorced, but divorce does happen to **nice kids**. Divorce happens to about **one million** kids each year. It happens to kids who live on farms, in cities, and in the suburbs. (Pages 120-121, 146-151, 204-207)

FALSE BELIEF #7

If a kid does not tell his feelings or thoughts to anyone, they will just go away. The problem will just disappear or vanish.

TRUE STATEMENT

It is better for a kid to **share** his feelings with a teacher, parent, grandparent, counselor, psychologist, social worker, or a member of the clergy. A problem doesn't seem as big when it is shared and understood. (Pages 114-115, 184-197)

FALSE BELIEF #8

After the divorce there is a good chance the parents will reunite, remarry each other, and live together again as a family with the kids.

TRUE STATEMENT

Divorce records and studies indicate that divorced parents **very rarely** reunite, remarry each other, and live together again. However, parents can make new friends and be happy living apart. (Pages 136-139)

FALSE BELIEF #9

Some kids believe there is something wrong with them because they are confused and have many different feelings before, during, and after the divorce.

TRUE STATEMENT

Kids facing a divorce often feel lonely, angry, sad, guilty, unhappy, and confused. It is **normal** and natural for kids to have many different feelings and it **doesn't** mean something is wrong with them. Remember: Divorce is **not** the kid's fault and kids feel better when they share their feelings. (Pages 92-93, 146-151, 168-197)

FALSE BELIEF #10

Kids can solve their parents' problems and save their parents' marriage.

TRUE STATEMENT

Kids **can't** solve their parents' problems and they can't save their parents' marriage. These are adult problems the parents must face. Parents often talk with friends, counselors, psychologists, lawyers, and the clergy to help them with their problems. (Pages 138-139, 152-157)

FALSE BELIEF #11

After the divorce the kids have to become "grown up" and take the place of the "missing" parent.

TRUE STATEMENT

Just as kids can't solve their parents' problems, they can't take the place of the "missing" parent. Parents **can** take care of themselves. However, kids can sometimes give their parents a helping hand with odd jobs and chores around the house. (Pages 156-161)

FALSE BELIEF #12

When kids live with one parent it means they are "taking sides" and don't love the "missing" parent.

TRUE STATEMENT

Kids can live with one parent and it **doesn't** mean they are "taking sides"; kids can still love both parents. Also, showing love for one parent **doesn't** mean a kid dislikes the other parent. Providing a helping hand or writing a nice note are ways kids can show love. (Pages 128-129, 158-159, 198-201)

FALSE BELIEF #13

Kids who experience divorce cannot do well in school.

TRUE STATEMENT

Kids who experience a divorce sometimes have difficulty in school. When there is fighting and trouble at home, it is often difficult for kids to concentrate and pay attention in school. However, their ability to pay attention **will improve** as well as their grades as they learn to share their feelings and accept the divorce. (Pages 76-81, 188-189)

FALSE BELIEF #14

Some kids think if they see a counselor or psychologist, it means they are crazy.

TRUE STATEMENT

If a kid goes to an eye doctor for an eye exam, does that mean he or she is blind? Of course not! It only means he or she may have difficulty seeing. Counselors and psychologists are caring people who help kids and adults learn to **cope** with worries and problems, including divorce. (Pages 116-119, 140-141, 144-145, 162-163, 166-167, 184-185)

Introduction For Kids

Sometimes divorce happens to a family... and when it does, everyone's life changes.

This is a story about a family and divorce. It is about a boy named Mike, a girl named Annie, their mom and dad, and even their dog, Kaya. So it goes ...

When I was just about your age, only two kids in my entire class had divorced parents. Now I am a school psychologist and I work in many different schools. I often see six, seven and even more kids in a classroom who have divorced parents. That's quite a jump from the two kids in my class.

As a school psychologist I've had the chance to help and talk with hundreds of kids with divorced parents.These kids taught me many important things about divorce and themselves. I want to share with you some of the things I learned.

For instance, I learned that kids don't cause parents to get a divorce and kids can't save their parents' marriage, no matter how hard they may try. I also learned that kids are strong young people. They can learn to cope (handle, live with) with changes in their lives, even the divorce of their parents.

As you read this book, you will learn that you are

strong enough to cope, and it will show you how.

As you learn to cope with your parents' divorce, you will realize that you can be happy again and feel good about yourself. You will see, just like Mike and Annie, that divorce does, indeed, happen to the nicest kids!

Michael S. Prokop
School Psychologist

Hello, my name is Mike . . .

. . . and this is my younger sister Annie, with our dog, Kaya.

I am going to tell you a true story about my family.

In the beginning my family was happy. I was just little then, but I remember my family was happy.

We would often go swimming . . .

. . . shopping . . .

. . . have cookouts in the backyard . . .

. . . and sometimes go to the park.

Mom and Dad were happy then, as they would often go to the movies . . .

. . . and to dinner at a nice restaurant.

Sometimes they would just sit at home and talk or watch T.V.

Our family was filled with love and we felt happy.

There was plenty of love in my family. My heart felt happy.

Changes

2

Things started to change. Dad's boss at work told him there was more work to be done.

Dad began coming home from work later and later. He was always tired.

Mom also seemed to be tired and she didn't talk as much as she used to do.

Mom and Dad began spending less and less time together . . .

. . . and when they were together, they didn't talk much.

Sometimes it seemed they were pretending that the other person wasn't even there. That made me feel a little uneasy and nervous.

And when they did talk, it seemed they always ended up yelling and screaming. That really made me nervous.

I began thinking about the arguing and fighting while
I was in school.

It was often difficult for me to concentrate and pay attention in class. My grades went down.

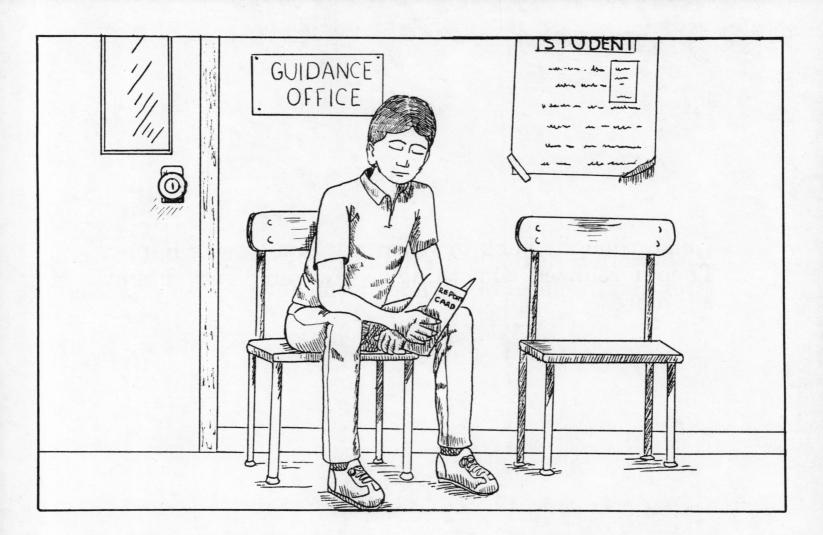

I also thought back to when my family was happy. Then I realized something; we weren't very happy anymore.

Our family wasn't happy and we didn't do things together anymore. Everyone felt nervous, upset, and sad. Things were different, things had changed.

I knew things were different and my parents seemed to keep fighting all the time. Then I heard the word DIVORCE.

I wasn't exactly sure what the word meant, but I thought it meant Mom and Dad wouldn't be living together anymore.

Finally, Mom and Dad said they were getting a divorce. They told us divorce meant the family would change; they wouldn't be married anymore.

They said, "It's not your fault, kids. We are unhappy with each other and just can't get along anymore. We love both of you very much."

I felt my heart begin to break when I heard the word divorce. My heart felt afraid and sad.

My sister and I felt many different feelings . . . sad, confused, angry and nervous. But my parents said things would be better, there would be less fighting and everyone would be happier.

My parents said Dad would move into an apart-
ment . . .

GREEN TREE
APARTMENTS

. . . and Annie and I would live with Mom at home.

After a few days I still felt confused and sad, but I noticed there wasn't as much fighting. That made me feel a little better.

I started doing things with my friends again and that helped me feel better.

Annie and I began to visit Dad every other weekend. That also helped me feel better.

My heart began to feel a little better. It was slowly beginning to mend.

Even though I was feeling a little better, I often felt unhappy and confused . . . I had many questions about divorce on my mind.

I told my mother about my confusion and we decided to visit a counselor.

A counselor is a nice person who listens to kids and adults and helps them understand their feelings, confusion, and worries.

While talking with the counselor I began to feel better. I learned many important things about divorce and myself.

I learned that divorce happens to many kids; over one million kids each year experience the divorce of their parents.

Divorce means my parents won't be married to each other and won't live together anymore.

However, it doesn't mean they don't love me any-more.

After a divorce, kids usually live with their moms, but some may live with their dads.

Also, just because one parent had to leave the home, it doesn't mean the "remaining" parent will abandon or leave the kids. Kids are taken care of!

Kids can live with one parent and it doesn't mean they are "taking sides" against the "missing" parent. Kids can still love both parents.

Also, showing love for one parent doesn't mean a kid dislikes the other parent.

I also learned that divorce changes the family and kids can be happy living with one parent. Some changes families and kids may face after a divorce include living on less money . . .

. . . moving to a new neighborhood . . .

. . . and changing schools and making new friends. These are changes some "divorced" families may face.

I also learned that divorce is usually forever and my parents won't get back together and remarry each other.

But, just as kids make new friends, parents can also make new friends and be happy living apart.

After our first visit with the counselor Annie and I realized we had learned many different things. We were beginning to understand divorce.

New Understandings

5

On our second visit with the counselor Annie and I
asked many questions. We learned that . . .

. . . kids are *not* the cause of the divorce . . .

. . . and parents do not get divorced because their kids have done something wrong . . .

. . . or have had bad thoughts.

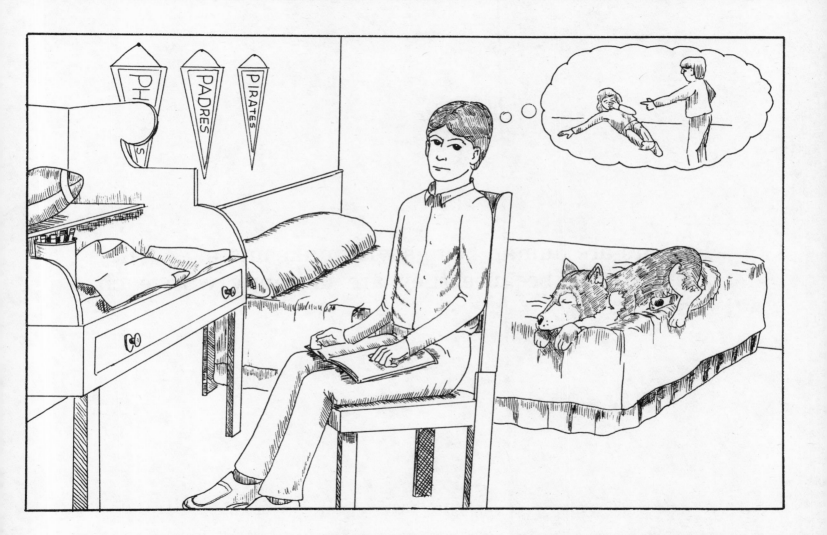

Parents are human beings who make mistakes. They get divorced because they are unhappy with each other . . .

. . . and can't work out their problems.

And kids can't solve their parents' problems, take care of their parents, or save their parents' marriage.

However, kids can give parents a helping hand with odd jobs and chores around the house.

GREEN TREE
APARTMENTS

But giving a helping hand *doesn't* mean kids have to become "grown up" and take the place of the "missing" parent. Parents *can* take care of themselves.

I was beginning to feel much better about myself as I learned about divorce. Divorce can be understood! Annie was feeling better too!

Feelings, Hope, and Happiness

6

On our last visit with the counselor Annie and I learned many important things about feelings, divorce, and ourselves.

We learned that it is all right for kids facing a divorce to feel many different feelings, such as disappointment and anger . . .

. . . fear . . .

. . . shame and embarrassment . . .

. . . sadness and loneliness . . .

. . . guilt . . .

. . . tension and confusion. These feelings are all normal and natural.

It is also normal for feelings to go way up and way down during the divorce.

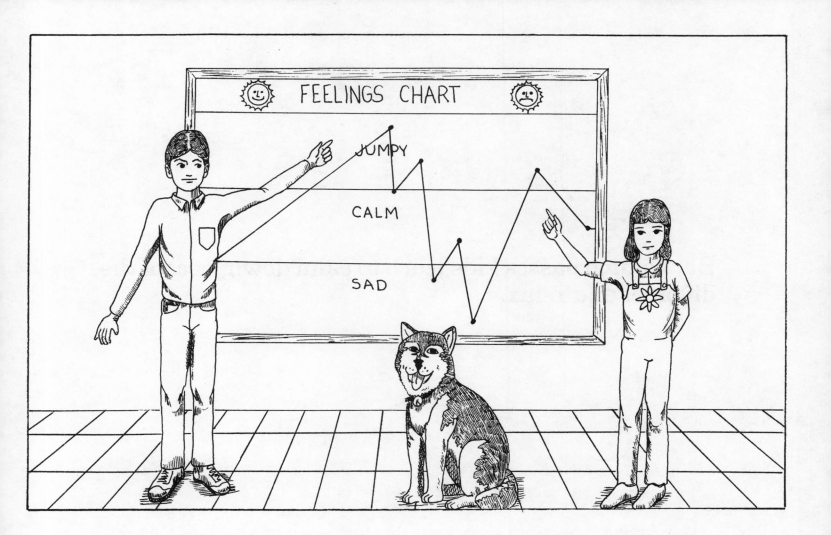

But as time passes kids learn to calm down, accept the divorce, and relax.

I also learned that I feel better when I share my feelings with a counselor . . .

. . . one or both of my parents . . .

. . . a concerned teacher . . .

. . . grandparents . . .

. . . or a member of the clergy. Sharing feelings helps kids feel better.

When I share my feelings, it feels like my problems and worries are cut in half.

Remember! It's O.K. to share feelings and problems.

Helping others . . .

. . . and showing love and concern also helps kids feel better.

Do you know the most important thing I learned?

Even though my parents are divorced, I'm a nice kid!
I can be happy again!

Divorce happens to the nicest kids!

MiKE

Mike

mike

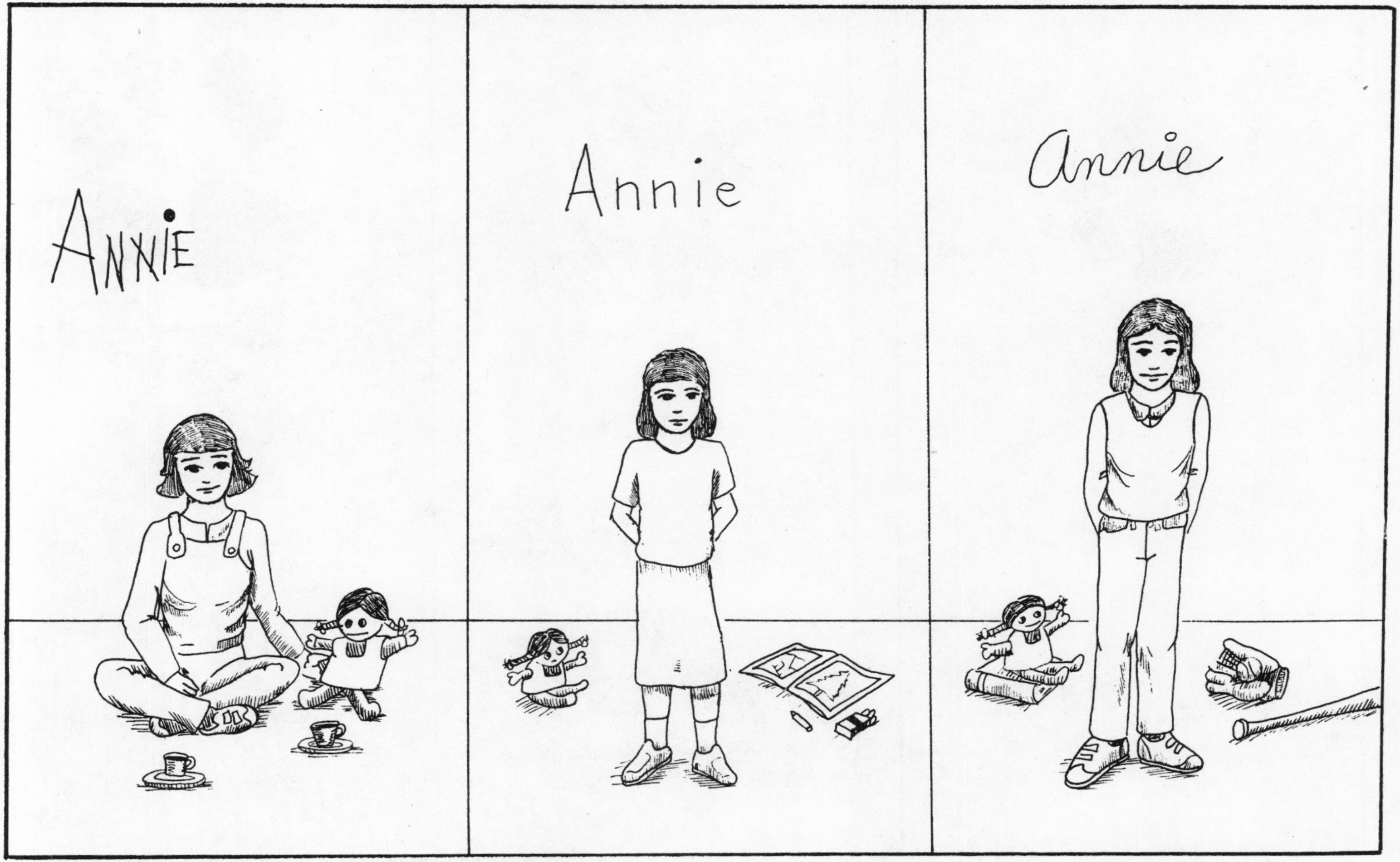
ANNIE
Annie
annie

GLOSSARY

anger - feeling extreme displeasure, feeling "mad"; kids often feel angry at their parents after a divorce.

Annie - a girl who learned to cope with the divorce of her parents; a nice kid; Mike's sister.

clergy - priest, nun, rabbi, minister and other religious people; nice people.

concentrate - to pay attention and direct your attention to one thing.

confusion - a feeling of not understanding what's going on; feeling helpless; sometimes leads to anger.

cope - to learn to understand, handle, and live with problems.

counselor - a nice woman or man who listens and helps kids cope with problems, including divorce.

disappointment - feeling sad or upset when things don't go as you hoped or expected they would.

divorce - a change in the family which means the parents won't be married and live together; parents who divorce very rarely get back together and remarry each other.

embarrassment - feeling ashamed and less that others; an uncomfortable feeling.

family - a dad, mom, and kids; many things can change a family such as divorce, illness, death, and older kids moving away to college or jobs.

fear - a feeling that comes when we don't understand or see what's going to happen next; fear can be overcome with understanding and knowledge.

guilt - a feeling that bad things happened because of you or something you did.

happy - a feeling of pleasure and joy; a feeling kids have when they know they can cope with problems.

Kaya - pronounced Kī-Yă; a Siberian Husky dog; according to an old Indian chief in Wyoming, Kaya means love.

kids - young nice human beings.

loneliness - feeling sad and alone; feeling separated from family and friends.

love - strong feelings of caring, affection, and tenderness.

*McDonalds - a fun place to eat good food; Mike and Annie often eat here with family and friends; great fries.

Mike - a boy who learned to cope with the divorce of his parents; a nice kid; Annie's brother.

nervous - feeling confused, jumpy, and uneasy; tense; to feel as if "butterflies" are in your stomach.

parents - nice people who fall in love, get married, have kids, and sometimes get divorced.

psychologist - a nice person like a counselor; listens and helps kids and adults cope with problems.

sadness - feeling unhappy and upset; downcast; depressed. Disappointments often cause kids to feel sad.

shame - strong feelings of regret and weakness; can be caused by guilt.

school - a place to learn things and have fun while learning; has teachers, a principal, and kids.

teachers - nice people who work in schools and help young human beings (kids) learn many different things; nice people to talk with and share feelings and worries.

tension - feeling uptight, nervous, and jumpy; confusion often causes tension.

work - things kids do in school to help them learn; things parents do at their jobs to earn money; work is sometimes fun.

worry - to think about a problem over and over again; worry doesn't help solve the problem and it sometimes causes kids and adults to feel anxious and nervous.

Bibliography

Ahron, C. B. (1980) Divorce: A crisis of family transition and change *Family Relations,* 4, 533-540.

Berg, B. and Kelly, R. (1979) The measured self-esteem of children from broken, rejected, and accepted families. *Journal of Divorce,* 2, 363-369.

Copeland, A. P. (1984) An early look at divorce: mother-child interactions in the first post-separation year. *Journal of Divorce,* 8, 22-30.

Davidoff, I. F. & Schiller, M. S. (1983) The divorce workshop as a crisis intervention: A practical model. *Journal of Divorce,* 6:4, 36-54.

Guidubaldi, J. Perry, J. D., Cleminshaw, H. K. and McLaughlin, C. S. (1983) The impact of parental divorce on children: report of the nationwide NASP study. *School Psychology Review,* 12, 300-323.

Hetherington, E. M. (1979) Divorce: A child's perspective. *American Psychologist,* 34, 851-858 .

Hetherington, E. M., Cox, M., & Cox R. (1978) The aftermath of divorce. In J. H. Stevens, Jr., & M. Mathews (Eds.). *Mother-child, father-child relations* (p. 149-170). Washington, D.C.: National Association for the Education of Young Children.

Hodges, W. F. and Bloom, B. L. (1984) Parents report of children's adjustment to marital separation: a longitudinal study. *Journal of Divorce,* 8, 33-50.

Jacobson, D. S. (1978) The impact of marital separation/divorce on children. 1. Parent/child separation and child adjustment. *Journal of Divorce,* 1, 341-459.

Kurdek, L. A. (1981) An integrative perspective on children's divorce adjustment. *American Psychologist,* 36, 856-866.

Kurdek, L. A. (1983) *Children and divorce.* San Francisco: Jossey-Bass.

Kurdek, L. A., Blisk, D., & Siesky, A. E. (1981) Correlates of children's long-term adjustment to their parent's divorce. *Developmental Psychology,* 17, 565-579.

Kurdek, L. A., & Siesky, A. E. (1980) Children's perceptions of their parents' divorce. *Journal of Divorce,* 3, 339-378.

Kurdek, L. A., & Siesky, A. E. (1980) The effects of divorce on children: The relationship between parent and child perspectives. *Journal of Divorce,* 4, 85-99.

Longfellow, C. (1979) Divorce in context: Its impact on children. In G. Levinger & O. C. Moles (Eds.). *Divorce and separation: Context, causes, and consequences* (pp. 287-306). New York: Basic Books.

Salts, C. J. & Zongker, C. E. (1983) Effects of divorce counseling groups on adjustment and self concept. *Journal of Divorce,* 6:4, 55-68.

Spanier, G. and Casto, R. (1979) Adjustment to separation and divorce: An analysis of 50 case studies. *Journal of Divorce,* 2, 241-253.

Stolberg, A. L., & Anker, J. M. (1984) Cognitive and behavioral changes in children resulting from parental divorce and consequent environmental changes. *Journal of Divorce,* 7, 23-41.

Stolberg, A. L. and Garrison, K. M. (1985) Evaluating a primary prevention program for children of divorce. *American Journal of Community Psychology,* 13, 111-124.

Wallerstein, J. S. (1983) Children of divorce: The psychological tasks of the child. *American Journal of Orthopsychiatry,* 53, 530-243.

Wallerstein, J. S. and Kelly, J. B. (1980) Surviving the Breakup: *How Children and Parents Cope with Divorce.* New York: Basic Books.

Warren, N. J., Grew, R. S., & Konanc, J. T. (1983) Parenting after divorce: Evaluation of preventive programs for divorcing families. *Resources in Education,* December, 1983. ED #232101.

Warren, N. J. and Ingrid, A. A. (1984) Educational groups for single parents: the parenting after divorce programs. *Journal of Divorce,* 18, 79-95.

FOR MORE INFORMATION

DIVORCE HAPPENS TO THE NICEST KIDS
A Self-Help Book for Kids and Adults

Written by School Psychologist Michael S. Prokop, explains divorce in a positive and reassuring manner. It concisely disproves fourteen irrational false beliefs concerning divorce that often cause children and adolescents to feel anxious, guilty, nervous and depressed. It takes the reader, step-by-step, from "False Belief" to "True Statement" as it discusses such critical issues as causes of divorce, parental problems and remarriage, living with one parent, concentration difficulties and academic regression, understanding emotions and conflicting feelings, and more.

© 1986   224 pages   Bibliography   Glossary   6"x9"   Illustrated
Hardcover   ISBN 0-933879-25-3 $18.95
Sofcover   ISBN 0-933879-26-1 $11.95

KIDS' DIVORCE WORKBOOK

This workbook is designed to complement the text as it helps kids understand their parents' divorce and themselves. Helps kids feel better about themselves as they become more aware of their positive aspects and inner strengths. Successfully used by the author to help kids in group and individual counseling. 96 pages   ISBN 0-933879-27-X $6.45

DIVORCE, CONFIDENCE, AND RELAXATION: A Guide for Kids, audio cassette tape (Prokop)

This tape is designed to help kids increase their confidence levels as they learn about divorce, stress reduction, and relaxation. Successfully used in group and individual counseling to help kids relax, disprove their irrational false beliefs, and accept and cope with their parents' divorce.
ISBN 0-933879-31-8 $9.95

DIVORCE HAPPENS TO THE NICEST KIDS, audio cassette tape.

The author reads the text and after each chapter discusses the concepts of the chapter with "Mike and Annie," two children who have experienced their parents' divorce. This tape also includes a "Kids Quiz" that helps kids further understand the concepts presented in the book.
ISBN 0-933879-28-8 $9.95

PROKOP DIVORCE ADJUSTMENT INVENTORY (PDAI)

This four page inventory is designed to help counselors and psychologists diagnose children and adolescents' irrational false beliefs concerning their parents' divorce. This easy to use instrument includes 54 incomplete sentences, 10 true/false, and a summary item.

ISBN 0-933879-30-X $8.40 (pkg. of 20)

RELAXATION AND POSITIVE THINKING FOR ADULTS*, audio cassette tape (Prokop)

The tape is designed to help adults focus on their positive aspects as they learn to cope with disturbing thoughts and stress. It also offers relaxation exercises that have been successfully used to help adults learn to relax, energize themselves, and enjoy life.
ISBN 0-933879-29-6 $9.95

* This tape has been successfully used with kids (10 and older.)

HELPING CHILDREN AND ADOLESCENTS COPE WITH DIVORCE: A Guide for Counselors, Teachers, and Parents audio cassette tape

In this lecture, which has been presented on a national level, Michael S. Prokop, consulting psychologist, addresses divorce research findings, factors in childrens' and adolescents' positive and poor adjustments to divorce, and irrational false beliefs influencing their reactions to divorce. Offers numerous practical suggestions with case studies to illustrate each false belief. An excellent resource for your professional library.   ISBN 0-933879-32-6 $9.95

Why Every School, Agency, Church and Counselor Needs A Comprehensive Divorce Adjustment Program:

1. Children and adolescents often react to their parents' divorce with severe behavioral, developmental, and academic regression.

2. Over one million children each year experience the divorce of their parents and another five hundred thousand will experience the separation of their parents.

3. Research indicates that four out of every ten children in America's classrooms will experience the divorce of their parents.

4. Over 12 million children under 18 currently have divorced parents.

5. Research indicates that a child's teacher is often the main support system at the time of his/her parents' divorce.

6. Children often react to divorce with unhealthy feelings of anxiety, anger, nervousness, confusion, guilt, loneliness, depression, and embarrassment.

7. These unhealthy feelings are often caused by false beliefs that children have about divorce, i.e., the divorce was their fault; no one will take care of them; they can't be happy living with one parent; their parents will get back together and remarry each other; they cannot do well in school; and more.

8. On "Childhood Trama Scales " divorce was second only to parental death as a cause of stress, anxiety, and depression.

9. The way teachers and counselors handle the divorce process directly affects the child's stress and anxiety levels.

THE DIVORCE GROUP COUNSELING PROGRAM

This unit includes everything necessary for a guidance counselor or psychologist to successfully conduct an eight week kids' divorce group. Includes a "weekly outline" with processing questions, parent permission forms, participation certificates, seven copies of **Divorce Happens to the Nicest Kids,** seven copies of **Kids' Divorce Workbook,** one package of the **PDAI,** and one copy of each audio cassette (4) listed. Successfully used in schools and clinics nationwide.

ISBN 0-933879-34-2 $164.95   Save over $30.50

KIDS' CONFIDENCE AND CREATIVITY KIT

8½"x11" Written and designed by School Psychologist Michael S. Prokop along with a school counselor and three classroom teachers. This kit includes "35 blackline masters" that may be reproduced and utilized by teachers and counselors to improve their students confidence and creativity levels. Highly recommended for upper elementary and middle school students.
ISBN 0-933879-33-4 $8.95

* Satisfaction Guaranteed *

ORDER FORM
Alegra House Publishers
Post Office Box 1443- P
Warren, Ohio 44482
(216) 372-2951

* Satisfaction Guaranteed *

Please send me the following materials:

_____ copies of **Divorce Happens to the Nicest Kids, A Self Help Book**
for Kids and Adults (Hard Cover) .... @ 18.95 each _____

_____ copies of **Divorce Happens to the Nicest Kids, A Self Help Book**
for Kids and Adults (Soft Cover) .... @ 11.95 each _____

_____ copies of **Divorce Happens to the Nicest Kids**, audio cassette tape .... @ 9.95 each _____

_____ copies of **Kids' Divorce Workbook** .... @ 6.45 each _____

_____ copies of **Divorce, Confidence, and Relaxation: A Guide for Kids**, audio cassette tape .... @ 9.95 each _____

_____ packages of **Prokop Divorce Adjustment Inventory (PDAI)** (20 protocols per package) .... @ 8.40 each _____

_____ copies of **Relaxation and Positive Thinking for Adults**, audio cassette tape .... @ 9.95 each _____

_____ copies of **Helping Children and Adolescents Cope With Divorce: A Guide**
for Counselors, Teachers and Parents, audio cassette tape .... @ 9.95 each _____

_____ copies of **Kids' Confidence and Creativity Kit** .... @ 8.95 each _____

_____ units of **The Divorce Group Counseling Program** .... @ 164.95 each _____

SUB TOTAL _____

Shipping: 10% of order; $2.00 minimum charge _____

Ohio Residents: Please add 5% sales tax .... _____

TOTAL DUE _____

* I understand that I may return any item for a full refund within <u>120</u> days of purchase if not satisfied.*

Name: _____

Address: _____ Zip _____

I am enclosing payment in the amount of $_____ . I wish to pay by:

☐ Charge Card   ☐ Check   ☐ Money Order   ☐ Purchase Order # _____

VISA or MASTERCARD INFORMATION

☐ VISA   ☐ Mastercard   ☐ Expiration Date: _____ Charge Card No. _____

Please Charge $ _____ to my charge account. Signature _____